THE SAMI

OF NORTHERN EUROPE

DEBORAH B. ROBINSON

Lerner Publications Company • Minneapolis

**First American edition published in 2002
by Lerner Publications Company**

Published by arrangement with Times Editions
Copyright © 2002 by Times Media Private Limited

Lerner Publications Company
A division of Lerner Publishing Group
241 First Avenue North
Minneapolis, MN 55401 U.S.A.
Website address: www.lernerbooks.com

Series originated and designed by
Times Editions
An imprint of Times Media Private Limited
A member of the Times Publishing Group
1 New Industrial Road, Singapore 536196
Website address: www.timesone.com.sg/te

Series editors: Margaret J. Goldstein, Daphne Rodrigues
Series designers: Tuck Loong, Lynn Chin
Series picture researcher: Susan Jane Manuel

Library of Congress Cataloging-in-Publication Data
Robinson, Deborah B.
The Sami of Northern Europe / by Deborah B. Robinson
— 1st American ed.
p. cm. — (First peoples)
Includes bibliographical references and index.
Summary: Describes the history, modern and traditional cultural
practices and economies, geographic background, and ongoing
oppression and struggles of the Sami.
ISBN 0-8225-4175-0 (lib. bdg. : alk. paper)
1. Sami (European people)—Juvenile literature. [1. Sami
(European people)] I. Title. II. Series.
DL42.L36 R635 2002
948'.0049455—dc21   2001004237

Printed in Malaysia
Bound in the United States of America

1 2 3 4 5 6—OS—07 06 05 04 03 02

CONTENTS

WHO ARE THE SAMI?

The Sami are the indigenous people of Europe's far north. They live in the northern parts of Norway, Sweden, and Finland and on the Kola Peninsula in northwestern Russia. The first Sami came to these regions thousands of years ago. Some of them hunted reindeer and other animals. Others hunted whales and seals and fished along the seacoast. Some modern Sami make a living by herding, hunting, or fishing. But they also work at many other jobs. Some 70,000 Sami live in Norway; about 25,000 in Sweden; about 7,000 in Finland; and some 3,000 in Russia. In addition, as many as 30,000 people with Sami ancestry live in North America.

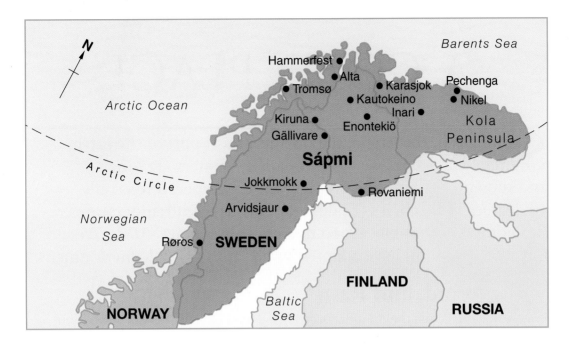

What's in a Name?

Sami is the name the people of Sápmi (Sami territory) call themselves. For a long time, non-Sami people called the Sami Lapps or Laplanders. This name comes from the Norwegian word *lapp*, which means "a patch of cloth." Non-Sami people looked down on the Sami for wearing patched, ragged clothing. Many people still call the Sami Lapps, not realizing that it is an insulting name. The Sami don't like being called Lapps. They prefer their own name.

The Sami are split into several groups, according to where they live. The Sea Sami live by the sea and make their living by fishing. The Eastern, or Skolt, Sami live along Finland's border with Russia. The Kola Sami live on the Kola Peninsula in Russia. Other groups are the Mountain Sami, Forest Sami, Lake Sami, River Sami, and South Sami. These different Sami groups don't have exactly the same culture and traditions.

A PEOPLE WITHOUT BORDERS

Land inhabited by the Sami is called Sápmi. Sápmi is not a country with borders and a government. Sami people are citizens of Norway, Sweden, Finland, or Russia. However, the Sami have had their own anthem since 1906 and their own flag (*right*) since 1986.

A COLD PLACE

Sápmi lies in the Arctic, the northernmost part of the earth. Arctic lands have very cold weather. Winters are long and snowy. In Sápmi, the average winter temperature is only 10 degrees Fahrenheit (-12 degrees Celsius). But temperatures sometimes drop as low as -60 degrees Fahrenheit (-51 degrees Celsius). The Sami have adapted to life in this tough environment.

Snow, Wind, and Rain

Winds blowing across the Atlantic Ocean bring a lot of rain and snow to Sápmi. Winter is the stormiest season. Snow falls from October to May. Some years, snow falls as late as July. Some places in Sápmi receive 12 feet (3.6 meters) of snowfall a year.

Below: Even in spring, some places in Sápmi are covered in snow.

Above: In summer, the sun lights up the sky even at night.

Cool Summer

Summers in Sápmi are cool and don't last long. The average summer temperature is only 57 degrees Fahrenheit (14 degrees Celsius). Because the summer season is short, plants have to grow quickly before the next winter season begins. Animals have to eat as much as they can in summer. They put on a layer of fat that will give them energy during the winter, when food is harder to find.

Light Nights

When the northern part of the earth tilts toward the sun, northern lands experience summer, with warm weather and long days. Arctic lands close to the North Pole receive the most sunshine in summer. In the far north of Sápmi, the sun never sets between mid-May and mid-July, and midnight can be almost as light as noon! The opposite occurs when the northern part of the earth tilts away from the sun. In the northernmost part of Sápmi, the sun never rises in December and most of January.

NORTHERN LIGHTS

On long winter nights, the northern lights (*right*), or aurora borealis, may shine over Sápmi. These lights occur when electrically charged particles from the sun hit the gases in the earth's atmosphere. This collision creates waves of beautiful moving lights in the sky. The northern lights are most often white or yellow-green. They can also be pink, blue, or violet. Red lights are rare and occur very high in the sky.

ARCTIC TERRAIN

Sápmi is home to a variety of landscapes, including mountains, forests, rocky coasts, and plains. Evergreen and birch trees grow in the forests. Other places, such as the mountains and coasts, have small plants and few or no trees.

Fells and Plateaus

Sápmi also has many fells and plateaus. A plateau, or tableland, is a raised, flat area of land. A fell is a rounded, treeless upland. The grasses that grow on fells provide good food for reindeer. Sami herders often take their reindeer onto fells to graze.

Below: Fells are found just south of the barren zone, called the tundra.

Above: The taiga makes up one-third of the world's forest area.

Taiga and Tundra

Forests in the southern part of the Arctic are known as the taiga. Because summers are so short and winters so cold, trees in the taiga don't grow very tall. The taiga is filled with swampy areas called bogs. North of the taiga lies a vast treeless plain called the tundra. The soil on the tundra is called permafrost. It stays frozen almost all year-round. Only the top layer of permafrost melts in summer.

FINGER-SHAPED WATERSCAPES

The coast of Norway has many fjords. A fjord (*right*) is a deep bay stretching between mountains or cliffs along a coast. On a map, fjords look like long thin fingers reaching into the land. Fjords are good places to fish for salmon and other fish. Many people think that fjords are among the most beautiful landscapes on earth.

ARCTIC PLANTS

Only the toughest plants are able to survive in Sápmi's windy, wintry weather. The cold, damp soil lacks many of the nutrients plants need to grow. Some plants, however, have found ways to flourish in the harsh Arctic landscape.

Evergreens and White Birches

The taiga contains mostly evergreen trees, such as pine, spruce, and fir trees. White birch trees and shrubs including willow and alders also grow in the forests of Sápmi. The forest floor is covered with lichens known as reindeer moss.

Below: Evergreen trees keep their leaves throughout the year. The waxy needle-shaped leaves do not lose too much water in winter.

ARCTIC BERRIES

Berries grow all over the tundra in late summer, and Sami families pick lots of them. Two of the tastiest Arctic berries are cloudberries and lingonberries. Lingonberries are small, dark red, and sour. Cloudberries (*right*), related to raspberries, are pinkish orange. They are flavorful but not very sweet. Cloudberries over reindeer milk cheese is a favorite dessert.

Shrubs, Lichens, and Mushrooms

Tall trees cannot grow in the tundra, because their long roots cannot reach deep into the permafrost for water and nutrients. Some small plants, however, such as the dwarf birch tree, can take root in the top layer of soil that thaws in summer. Grasses, small shrubs, mosses, and lichens also grow on the tundra. Edible mushrooms grow in the forests of central Sweden.

Endangered Tundra

Many human activities hurt the Arctic. When people walk or drive over permafrost in summer, they leave permanent tracks that scar the tundra. When people build towns, roads, and factories, they leave less and less room for animals and plants. When people mine for minerals and drill for oil, they pollute the land and poison the plants and the animals.

Left: Reindeer moss is a lichen. It grows in sandy soil and becomes spongy when wet and brittle when dry. It gets its name from the reindeer that use it for food.

ARCTIC ANIMALS

Bears, reindeer, and moose are the largest land animals in Sápmi. Smaller land animals include wolves, foxes, lemmings, lynx, otters, and beavers. Eagles, loons, beautiful songbirds, and many other kinds of birds build their nests in Sápmi. Seals, walruses, and fish swim in the seas. Many fish also live in Sápmi's lakes and rivers.

Reindeer and Moose

Reindeer are especially suited to living in cold places. Soft fur covers their bodies and even their noses. This fur traps a blanket of air, which protects the reindeer from the cold. The fur also acts like a life jacket, helping the reindeer float and swim easily. Reindeer are strong swimmers and often swim across wide, fast-flowing rivers and cold ocean bays. The wide, split hooves of the reindeer are perfect for walking across the snowy Arctic ground. The hooves act like snowshoes, helping the reindeer walk on snow and soft tundra. The hooves are also good for digging into snow for buried lichens and grasses.

Moose are much larger than reindeer. They can stand up to 7.5 feet (2.3 meters) tall at the shoulder and weigh up to 1,800 pounds (817 kilograms). Moose live in the taiga, where they like to munch on twigs and wade in bogs. Male moose have huge antlers stretching up to 6 feet (1.8 meters) across.

Left: Both male and female reindeer grow antlers.

Arctic Predators

Wolves and wolverines are predators—animals that eat other animals. Wolves were once plentiful in Sápmi. But over the years, Sami herders killed many wolves to protect their reindeer. Wolverines are fierce members of the weasel family. They can grow up to 40 inches (101 centimeters) long and weigh up to 70 pounds (32 kilograms). Wolverines hunt mostly at night. They usually eat berries, birds' eggs, dead animals, and small animals such as lemmings. But they sometimes attack larger animals such as reindeer calves.

Left: The wolverine has strong jaws capable of crushing bones.

Creatures of the Air and Sea

Sápmi is home to small songbirds and large birds of prey such as gyrfalcons, eagles, and rough-legged buzzards. Whales, walruses, seals, and fish live in the ocean waters around Sápmi. Rivers in the region are filled with fish such as Arctic char and Atlantic salmon. In summer, Sápmi is home to millions of insects, including mosquitoes and warble flies.

Right: An Atlantic salmon leaps out of the gushing waters of a fast-flowing river.

LEMMING MIGRATION

Lemmings are small relatives of mice. They live in large groups called colonies. Every three to five years, hundreds or even thousands of lemmings migrate in search of new food supplies. They walk through towns and swim across lakes. Some of the lemmings are eaten by foxes and other predators along the way. There is a myth that lemmings commit mass suicide by jumping over cliffs into the sea. There is no truth to this myth.

DWELLERS OF THE ANCIENT ARCTIC

Archaeologists—scientists who study ancient cultures—think that thousands of years ago, the ancestors of present-day Sami lived on the western side of the Ural Mountains, in northwestern Russia. More powerful, warlike people probably chased the Sami ancestors away from the Urals, toward northern Finland, Sweden, and Norway. Archaeologists have found evidence suggesting that the Sami ancestors arrived on the coast of Norway around 9000 B.C.

Below: Some rock carvings found in Alta are between 2,500 and 5,500 years old. They give archaeologists clues about the way early Sami lived.

Above: Sami hunters made bear traps from wood and stone.

Fishing and Hunting

Early Sami caught fish, whales, seals, and walruses in the Norwegian Sea. They set out in wooden boats that were made from overlapping boards bound with sinew, or animal tendon. Early Sami fishermen used animal horn and slate, a kind of rock, to make fishhooks and harpoons. Inland, early Sami hunters trapped reindeer, moose, bears, and beavers. Their weapons were wooden spears, bows and arrows, and knives.

The Beginning of Herding

About one thousand years ago, the Sami stopped hunting reindeer and began to herd them. This way, the Sami always had plenty of animals to provide meat, milk, hides, and antlers. To gather the herds, Sami hunters chased reindeer into enclosures made of wood and brush. They killed some of the reindeer for meat and hides. But the hunters also saved some of the reindeer and tamed them. When wild reindeer saw the tamed herds, they felt safe and joined the animals in captivity.

SAMI NOMADS

Early Sami reindeer herders (*right*) were nomads—they moved from place to place. Sometimes, they moved to find good grazing lands for their reindeer. Other times, they followed wild reindeer, hoping to catch them and enlarge their herds. The herders also moved to avoid predators that endangered baby reindeer or to escape insects that bothered the herd.

FOREIGN INVADERS

About two thousand years ago, people south of Sápmi began to move north into Sami lands. Some of these visitors traded with the Sami. Others fought with them. In A.D. 98, travelers from the south reported meeting the Sami, whom they called Finni. In A.D. 600, some visitors noted that the Sami traveled on skis. Some of these newcomers eventually settled in Sápmi for good. They often took the best lands for their farms and herds and pushed the Sami onto poorer lands farther north. It became harder and harder for the Sami to live off the land.

Below: Viking explorers sailed the rough seas to reach new northern lands.

Viking Newcomers

The Vikings were people who lived south of Sápmi in Norway, Denmark, and Sweden. In 890, a Viking chieftain named Ottar demanded taxes from the Sami. Instead of money, the Sami paid with furs, duck feathers, and other products. The Vikings and the Sami sometimes exchanged ideas and influenced each other. For instance, the Sami helped the Vikings build their boats. Sami and Viking boats looked similar—wide in the middle and curved upward at the front and back. Also, some Sami words are similar to words in Norse, the language of the Vikings.

Above: Sami boats have pointed tips, similar to Viking boats.

Christian Missionaries

Along with the Vikings, missionaries arrived in Sami lands. The missionaries were religious teachers who worked to convert people of other faiths to Christianity. The Sami had their own religion, filled with the spirits of nature. But the missionaries did not respect this religion. They called the Sami heathens—an insulting name for non-Christians. The missionaries built a number of churches in Sami territory. One of them, located in Tromsø on the northwestern coast of Norway, was named Saint Maria Next to the Heathens.

RELIGION UNDER ATTACK

Christian leaders gradually began to attack the Sami's spiritual beliefs and practices. In 1685, the Christians burned sacred Sami objects. They even burned to death some Sami spiritual leaders. They tried to force the Sami to follow Christian beliefs. This picture shows some Sami being baptized by a Christian priest. They had to give up their sacred drums (*bottom left*) when they became Christians.

STOLEN HOMELAND

European rulers claimed parts of Sápmi as their own territory. They sent soldiers into Sápmi to collect taxes and enforce laws. Many of these laws were unfair to the Sami. The Sami had few rights and were gradually pushed out of their own homeland.

Cruel Treatment

New rulers and intruders were often cruel to the Sami. In 1635, Swedish soldiers punished Sami who refused to work in silver mines at Nasafjäll. In 1852, Norway's border with Finland was closed, blocking a traditional Sami travel route. During World War II (1939–1945), German troops burned buildings in Sápmi to slow down their Russian pursuers. After the war, the Sami had to rebuild their towns.

Below: The town of Hammerfest was rebuilt after World War II.

Going to America

People from the south kept pushing the Sami farther north. Many Sami gave up herding and farming to become miners and loggers. In the 1860s, when copper mines in Norway closed down, many Sami families went hungry. Unemployment forced thousands of Sami to leave for the United States. Many settled in Massachusetts, Michigan, Wisconsin, Minnesota, the Dakotas, and Washington State. Some Sami migrated to Alaska.

Above: Unfair treatment by foreigners forced many Sami to leave their homeland.

Forced to Fit In

Sami who stayed in Sápmi faced further discrimination. The government put pressure on the Sami to fit in with mainstream society. In Norway, Sami children were not allowed to speak their own language in school. In Sweden, many Sami did not have the same rights and job opportunities as other Swedish people did.

Right: Sami schoolchildren in the 1950s and 1960s had no chance to study in the Sami language.

LOSING THEIR CULTURE

Eventually, many Sami were forced to stop speaking their own language and practicing their old traditions. They were taught that they were not as good as other Europeans. They were given Christian names to replace their Sami names. Sometimes, Sami who moved to the United States played down their Sami heritage in favor of their national Scandinavian identities.

FIGHT FOR POWER

I n the early 1900s, the Sami began to unite and fight for their rights. They set up their first organization in 1904. Sami in Norway, Sweden, and Finland formed the Nordic Sami Council in

1956. Now called the Saami Council, it works for fair treatment of the Sami. Sami organizations have earned modern Sami full citizenship in their home countries, but they still struggle over cultural, land, and resource rights.

Above: Saami Council chairman Pekka Aikio (*left*) sits with Finnish president Tarja Halonen (*center*).

Below: A Sami herder demonstrates against unfair treatment of the Sami.

Above: This hydroelectric dam in Sápmi uses the power of a river to create energy.

Protests at Alta

In 1970, the Norwegian government decided to build a hydroelectric dam on a river near Alta in northern Norway. The Sami objected to the project, because the dam would flood their grazing land. However, construction went ahead. Sami and non-Sami protesters tried to stop the project by chaining themselves to the bulldozers. They were arrested and fined, and construction continued. However, people in Norway and other countries began to notice the Sami and to support their fight for political power.

A Voice in Politics

The Sami later began to form their own parliaments. Norway created the first Sami parliament in 1989. Sweden followed in 1993, and Finland in 1996. Sami people elect their parliament members, who talk about problems facing the Sami and how to solve them. The Sami in Russia do not yet have their own parliament.

Right: A Russian Sami gives a speech, while holding up a picture of the Sami flag.

A NEW COUNCIL

In 1996, a new international group was formed to handle concerns of northern peoples. Called the Arctic Council, it has members from the Saami Council and other indigenous groups and representatives from the governments of Canada, Denmark, Finland, Iceland, Norway, Russia, Sweden, and the United States. The Arctic Council tries to improve the lives of people in northern areas and to solve problems facing the Arctic environment.

HERDING REINDEER

In the past, reindeer herding was a major part of Sami life. Herding families drank reindeer milk and ate reindeer stew, reindeer sausage, and reindeer milk cheese. They made clothing and tents from reindeer hide and tools from reindeer antlers. Some modern Sami families still herd reindeer for a living. But they also hold other jobs to bring in enough money for the family.

Herders at Work

Sami families work together to tend their reindeer. The herders take turns circling the animals, keeping them together and watching for predators. Dogs help the herders in their work. In the fall, the herders kill some reindeer for meat. In spring, they cut little notches into the ears of newborn calves in order to identify them. In the old days, herders milked reindeer in summer and used most of the milk to make cheese. The largest herds then included several thousand animals.

Below: A Sami woman dries reindeer hides in the sun.

Below: A traditional Sami herder moves on wooden skis. His reindeer is harnessed to a wooden sled.

Tools for Herding

Sami herders use knives to slice rope, slaughter reindeer, make earmarks, cut sticks, and slice food. They carry walking staffs made from wood or antler and use leather rope lassos to capture reindeer. They travel on sleds and skis.

Modern Herders

Modern herders use the best new technology in the reindeer business. They communicate using cell phones and travel on snowmobiles. Present-day herds include only about one hundred to three hundred reindeer. Herders keep some reindeer meat, hides, and antlers for their own use and sell the rest for money.

Left: A modern Sami herder zooms around on a snowmobile.

WATERPROOF TENTS

A traditional Sami tent, or *lavvu*, was made from reindeer hide. Some modern Sami still live in reindeer hide tents. But most modern Sami tents are made from heavy waterproof cloth. Most modern herders also have small cabins or houses near their pastures. After a cold day on the tundra, these houses are warmer and more comfortable than tents.

COMBINING OLD AND NEW

In modern times, less than 10 percent of Sami people herd reindeer for a living. Instead, most Sami people hold jobs as miners, loggers, tour guides, shopkeepers, doctors, bus drivers, teachers, and government officials. But Sápmi is far away from big cities. Jobs are sometimes hard to find, and many Sami don't earn a lot of money at their jobs. Meat and fish that they can catch, hunt, or get in trade are very important to the Sami.

Left: A Sami tailor uses an electric sewing machine to make traditional clothing.

Mining and Logging

Mining and logging companies are the biggest businesses in most parts of Sápmi. They often pay their workers better than other businesses, but they also cause problems in Sápmi. For instance, mining pollutes the air, land, and water. Logging destroys trees and harms the animals living in the forests. Reindeer rely on forest plants for food. So the logging business hurts reindeer and reindeer herders, too.

Left: Dried cod. Sami fishermen catch cod and other types of fish.

Fishing

In coastal areas, many Sami people work full-time as commercial fishermen. They fish from large modern boats and sell their catches for money. Other Sami people work at fish farms, where fish such as salmon are raised in human-made ponds. Some Sami don't work in the fishing industry, but catch fish for their own home use. They like fishing as well as eating fish.

HUNTING AND FISHING RIGHTS

Many outsiders come to Sápmi to hunt and fish. Anglers eager to catch Arctic char, Atlantic salmon, trout (*right*), and other fish will pay as much as $1,200 a day for fishing licenses and guides. Foreign anglers and hunters bring lots of money to Sápmi, but many Sami want them kept away. The Sami depend on hunting and fishing for their traditional food. They do not want outsiders killing off supplies of fish and animals.

ENCOURAGING TOURISM

Many tourists visit Sápmi to hunt and fish, to enjoy the fjords and forests, and to learn about Sami culture. As more and more visitors come to Sápmi, roads, hotels, restaurants, and other facilities have to be built. This construction provides jobs for the Sami. Also, tourists spend a lot of money on food, souvenirs, and events like snowmobile safaris and reindeer sled tours. Tourism helps the economy of Sápmi. But it also brings problems.

Below: Tourists take a rest on the steps of a hotel in Sápmi.

Above: Dolls like these are sold as "Sami," but they are often made in China.

Fakes and Frauds

Tourists in Sápmi don't always get to experience real Sami culture. Non-Sami people may fool tourists by wearing Sami clothes and serving snacks in Sami-style tents. They often sell dolls and other "Sami" items without the permission of Sami people. The Sami don't make any money from these sales.

Selling Sami Culture

Many Sami people sell homemade handicrafts to tourists or welcome visitors into traditional tents for a Sami snack or meal. Visitors get to taste Sami specialties such as reindeer stew and reindeer tongue sandwiches, while sitting on reindeer hides around a fire. But not all Sami people like the idea of selling their culture this way. They want to be treated as human beings, not tourist attractions.

Right: Markets in Sápmi sell a variety of Sami-style handicrafts.

A MORE OPEN PLACE

Sápmi was once isolated and remote. But in recent years, roads have been built, logging and mining operations have been set up, and people from southern areas have built summer homes in Sápmi. These activities have hurt Sápmi and Sami culture. For instance, fast-moving cars kill more and more reindeer every year.

SAMI AT HOME

For generations, Sami families camped in communities called *sii'da*. Families in a sii'da herded reindeer together and migrated at the same time. Modern Sami no longer live in big nomadic groups, but they still refer to Sami communities as sii'da.

Food for All

The migratory sii'da changed in size during the year, depending on how much food was available. In winter, when food was hard to find, the sii'da was small, with only one to three families sharing scarce resources. A summertime sii'da could have about one hundred people in twenty to thirty families. Food was plentiful in summer, so it was easy to find enough to feed a big group.

Below: Sami men cook fresh fish over a lavvu fire.

Above: A Sami toddler sits snugly in a little sled.

Babies and Children

Sami babies were traditionally bundled into wooden cradle boards lined with moss. Leather bands held them safe in the cradle, while they played with bands of beads and buttons. Older children had chores, such as cutting wood and tending the fire.

Home Sweet Lavvu

To make a lavvu, one or two family members stretched reindeer hides over a frame of poles. The family then covered the ground inside with reindeer hides, fur side up, so that they could sit and sleep comfortably. The family built a fire in the center of the lavvu and hung kettles and pots from the frame poles. When it was time to move camp, the family took the lavvu apart and loaded it onto a sled.

MOVING HOUSE

When a sii'da moved, everyone traveled on foot, skis, or sleds. Old-style sleds were shaped like small boats. The sleds were loaded with cargo and harnessed to reindeer. Riders used reins to guide the reindeer. The reindeer carried cargo, and sometimes children, on their backs. Modern Sami pack their belongings on snowmobiles as well as sleds when they travel (*right*).

CITIES AND TOWNS

During the 1900s, most Sami people gave up jobs like herding and farming. They moved to towns, where they took regular paying jobs and sent their children to school. Modern Sami people live much like other Europeans. They live in houses, drive cars, and use computers and telephones. Technology has helped bring the communities of Sápmi closer to the rest of the world.

Left: Tromsø in Norway has many colorful houses.

Urban Centers

Sápmi has many towns and several cities. Tromsø in Norway is a coastal city of 56,000 people. The biggest industry there is fishing. Rovaniemi in Finland is a big tourist center on the Arctic Circle and is home to 35,000 people. Other Sami communities include Jokkmokk and Arvidsjaur in Sweden, Alta and Røros in Norway, and Inari and Enontekiö in Finland. Many non-Sami live in Sápmi. In fact, there are more non-Sami than Sami in most towns.

Below: The Artikum Museum in Rovaniemi, Finland, holds exhibitions of Sami culture.

Above: Sami girls in Sápmi wear traditional clothes to school.

Higher Education

Some schools and universities in Sápmi teach people about Sami life. Students at the University of Tromsø in Norway can choose to study fishing, Sami culture, and other subjects. The Sami Institute in Kautokeino, Norway, does research on Sami language and society. Sami College, also in Kautokeino, offers classes in reindeer breeding and Sami handicrafts. Many students at the University of Sápmi in Rovaniemi, Finland, learn about the Arctic environment and culture.

SANTA'S VILLAGE

Santa Claus is a major tourist attraction in Rovaniemi, Finland. The town has built him a village, complete with reindeer and souvenir shops. Visitors to Rovaniemi can meet Santa any day of the year, but most choose Christmas. Every Christmas, hundreds of people fly to Rovaniemi from cities all over Europe to be as close to Santa—and his Christmas gifts (*left*)—as possible.

SAMI STYLE

Modern Sami usually wear ordinary clothes like those worn by people in the rest of Europe and in the United States. But Sami people sometimes dress in traditional outfits called *gakti*, especially on special occasions like indigenous holidays, gatherings, and weddings. Those who work for groups like the Saami Council usually wear gakti to work.

Gakti Dress

Sami from different regions wear different colors and designs. Women in most areas wear dresses made from boiled wool, belted at the waist and decorated with colorful bands and ribbons. Sami women sometimes wear reindeer skin leggings. Some wear colored shawls around their shoulders. Some wear tall fur hats, sometimes stuffed with grass for extra warmth.

Sami men wear shorter tunics, also belted at the waist. They wear fur parkas over their tunics when the weather gets very cold. Some wear hats with four points on top. Sami people often wear clothing made from polar fleece and modern fabrics. However, reindeer-hide clothing is coming back into fashion.

Left: A Lake Sami man wears a traditional four-pointed Sami hat.

Winter Boots

Traditional Sami winter boots are made of reindeer hide and have pointed, curly toes. The curled-up toes were especially useful in the days of wooden skis, as they could be slipped beneath ski straps to hold the skier's feet in place. Some Sami winter boots are short, and some are tall. Some can even be adjusted to different heights. The boots are stuffed with grass for added protection from the winter cold.

Above: Curly toed Sami boots come in different sizes.

Right: The Sami wear fur coats in very cold weather.

Making Clothing

Sami women are in charge of making new clothes for their families. They use a wooden bar with a metal attachment to scrape and soften the reindeer hides. They use small looms made of wood and antler to weave belts and decorative bands. When making grass insulation for boots and hats, Sami women use a hackle—a comb with metal teeth—to remove seeds from the grass.

RINGS AND RATTLES

Traditional Sami outfits are decorated with beautiful silver and gold pins (*left*) and jingling silver and brass coins or disks. The Sami sometimes wear jewelry that holds tiny jingling rings. Sami families make their own version of the baby rattle by hanging bunches of jingling rings over their babies' cradles. The jingling of the rings helps keep evil spirits away from the babies.

MODERN LIVING

I n some ways, Sami communities resemble other towns in Europe. People there drive cars, talk on the telephone, and go to work or to school. For town and city Sami, the days of living on the tundra in tents have passed. Yet they still make time for traditional activities, such as picking berries, catching fish, and helping their relatives tend farms and herds.

Below: This apartment block in Sápmi shows modern architectural design.

Above: Stores in Sápmi sell Sami music and videos.

Reviving Sami Culture

In recent years, the Sami have worked hard to revive their culture. Some Sami schoolchildren learn the Sami language, in addition to the main language of their home country, such as Swedish or Finnish. Governments have also given money to Sami cultural projects, such as radio and television shows broadcast in the Sami language. Some Sami youths create their own radio shows and websites in the Sami language, English, and the languages of their countries.

City Life

Many Sami no longer live in Sápmi. They have moved south to big cities like Oslo in Norway, Stockholm in Sweden, and Helsinki in Finland. Many Sami are attracted to big cities like these, where there are more jobs than Sápmi can offer. Sami who live in big cities live modern lifestyles, but they still practice their old Sami traditions and usually maintain close ties with their homeland, Sápmi.

Right: Modern Sami teenagers pay attention to fashion trends.

ON THE AIR AND ONLINE

Radio Sápmi is a radio and television station that broadcasts shows in the Sami language. Sami children have even worked on some of these shows, writing the stories, acting, and running the cameras and other equipment. The station also has an Internet website and produces web pages for children and teenagers.

ART AND MUSIC

Traditionally, the Sami had no written language. Instead, they communicated through painting, carving, storytelling, and singing. Modern Sami artists still express themselves in these ways. Some Sami musicians perform the *joik*—an old style of singing.

Ancient Artists

Along Norway's coast, there are rock drawings of animals, the sun, hunters with bows and arrows, and other scenes. Most of these pictures date from 1500 to 2000 B.C. and were possibly drawn by the ancestors of the Sami. The ancient artists drew on rock using a paint made of red ocher, a kind of earth. Later, Sami artists carved designs on reindeer antler and made beautiful knife handles and cases. Modern-day collectors prize old Sami knives for their quality and workmanship.

Below: Modern Sami paintings show reindeer and other aspects of Sami culture.

Preserving the Past

Modern Sami artists often copy old designs when making new arts and crafts. They paint pictures of reindeer and the sun, similar to those found on ancient rock carvings and sacred drums. Sami silversmiths make beautiful jewelry based on ancient objects and designs. Modern Sami artists frequently use materials that their ancestors used, such as wood and reindeer hide and antler. Knife handles and cases and drinking cups are often made from birch wood or reindeer antler. These materials are readily available in Sápmi.

Above: Sami cups are made from birch wood. Herders sometimes hang cups on their belts.

Joik Singing

A joik is a chant that honors people, events, or nature. The Sami perform the joik on special occasions such as weddings and funerals. They sometimes sing a joik to a sweetheart or rival. A joik expresses feelings of sorrow, hate, joy, or love. Sometimes two men hold a contest to see who can chant a cleverer, sweeter, or more spirited joik. The joik has traditionally been passed down from generation to generation by word of mouth.

SAMI CELEBRITIES

Nils-Aslak Valkeapää is a modern writer, singer, and actor. He has appeared in several films, including *Pathfinder*, the first film ever made in the Sami language. His popular recordings introduced the non-Sami world to the joik. Mari Boine (*right*) has attracted both Sami and non-Sami fans with her mix of the joik and jazz and rock music. She writes songs, plays musical instruments, and dances on stage during live concerts.

SPEAKING SAMI

Sami people speak nine different languages. Each one differs a little from the others. The main language is Northern Sami, spoken by about 75 percent of Sami people. The Sami languages contain a few words of Norwegian, Finnish, and Russian, introduced by early foreign traders in Sápmi.

Below: Two Sami women enjoy an outdoor chat while fishing.

History of the Language

The Sami languages are related to northern Russian tribal languages and to Hungarian, Estonian, and Finnish. Originally, the Sami did not have an alphabet. But when missionaries and other outsiders came to Sápmi, they wrote Sami words in foreign alphabets. Modern writers create books and poems in the Sami languages. Some tell old tales. Others write new stories.

SAMI SPELLING

Sami words are generally easy to pronounce—you say every letter. The only trouble is, some words are very long, with complicated spelling. For instance, the city name Kautokeino is spelled Guovdageaidnu in Sami. In addition, the Sami alphabet has seven more letters than we have in English. Even more confusing, Eastern Sami uses Russian letters, or Cyrillic. These letters look nothing like those of our Roman alphabet.

Learning the Language

For many years, the Sami languages were outlawed. The Sami were forced to speak Swedish, Norwegian, Finnish, or Russian. In modern times, only about one-third of Sami people speak their traditional languages. Some of these languages have almost disappeared. Only a few hundred people still know how to speak them. In the 1960s, the Sami began to revive their old languages. In school, modern Sami children often learn both Sami and the national language. Special Sami high schools are found in some Sápmi towns.

Above: This traffic sign in Sápmi has Finnish and English words.

Describing the Environment

The Sami languages are rich in words about animals, families, and the land. For instance, there are about four hundred words describing reindeer, according to size, color, age, antlers, fur, and other traits. Many Sami words also describe different kinds of snow, depending on when and how heavily it falls. Other words describe how fast a river flows.

Right: A Skolt Sami woman reads a religious book.

NATURE'S SPIRITS

Traditional Sami believe that spirits inhabit the natural world. The Sami also believe they can communicate with animals, the wind, and the sun. They treat all forms of nature with respect. This attitude helps the Sami survive in a harsh environment. They believe that people who do not respect nature will have trouble living off the land. The Sami sometimes offer jewelry or sacrifice reindeer to the spirits. This practice is meant to keep life in balance.

Right: The bones and antlers of sacrificed reindeer

Noaide and Ulda

The Sami believe that certain people have special powers. Called *noaide,* these people ask the spirits for help during hunting season and in times of hunger and sickness. In the past, because life was so tough in the cold climate of Sápmi, help from the noaide was very important. The Sami also believe that little people called *ulda* live underground. These beings can either help or harm people. If a herder leaves the ulda an offering, the creatures help take care of the herder's reindeer. But the ulda can also be harmful. They are said to steal babies and children. The Sami believe that the ulda taught them how to chant the joik.

Left: A *stalo* is a sacred rock.

40

Left: Finnish priests meet with a Sami herder (*center*) to discuss the translation of a prayer book into the Sami language.

A New Religion

Christian missionaries arriving in Sápmi in the 1200s thought the Sami religion was devil worship. They wanted the Sami to give up their old beliefs. The Christians replaced ancient Sami festivals with Christian holidays and often used force to make the Sami join their churches. Some modern-day Sami belong to the Laestadian branch of the Lutheran Church. This group conducts religious services in the Sami language. However, many Sami still practice their old religion. Some sacred Sami sites and objects can still be seen in Sápmi.

Right: A wooden church attended by a Sami Christian community

THE SACRED DRUM

To communicate with the spirits, the noaide used a sacred drum (*left*) covered with drawings of animals and mythical beings. A small piece of antler was placed on the drum. When the drum was beaten, the antler piece bounced around. According to where it landed, the noaide read a message from the spirits.

41

CELEBRATIONS

Ancient Sami held festivals to celebrate their relationship with nature. For instance, people celebrated when the sun returned to the sky in spring. Such ceremonies have become rare. Modern Sami often observe Christian holidays.

The Bear Ceremony

A big event was a bear hunt led by the noaide. When the hunters found a bear in its den, they walked around it and then killed it with their spears. As they carried the bear to camp, they chanted a joik for it. For three days, people honored the bear with ceremonies. They ate the bear and buried its bones. The bear ceremony slowly disappeared after the Christians arrived.

Below: Family events are occasions for Sami relatives to come together in celebration.

Above: A painting of the Sami bear ceremony. A successful ceremony was believed to help keep hunters safe the next year.

Getting Married

Sami weddings are happy family occasions. Everyone wears their finest traditional outfits. After the wedding ceremony, which is held in a church, people throw a party that might last for days. They enjoy lots of food and drink, and they talk and dance. Joik performers compete at the party, inventing joik after joik on the spot.

Above: Family members surround a newly married Sami couple. The bride and groom are dressed in their finest outfits, complete with silver brooches.

Modern Holidays

Easter is the biggest festival for modern Sami. They celebrate Easter by going to church and playing outdoor games. The Sami also celebrate other Christian holidays, such as Christmas, and nonreligious holidays, such as New Year. Midsummer, a major holiday, falls during the summer solstice, when the sun shines all night in Arctic lands. People build big bonfires and stay up late into the night to celebrate.

FUNERAL PARTIES

Early Sami did not bury their dead. They placed the body in a simple coffin, sled, or hollowed-out tree trunk and left it on an island or in a cave. The dead person's family threw a big party at the funeral. The Sami believed the family would have bad luck otherwise.

FUN AND GAMES

Sami pastimes come from generations of living in the outdoors. Many old activities, such as skiing and sledding, involved snow. Other pastimes, such as joik singing and storytelling, helped people entertain one another during long winter nights. Modern Sami still enjoy many traditional pastimes. They also like modern sports such as snowmobile racing and soccer.

Skiing: The Sami Invented It

The Sami invented skis thousands of years ago. They found that skiing was the best way to travel across snow. When Sami started to herd reindeer, they discovered an even faster way to travel on snow. Wearing their skis, they used reindeer or dogs to pull them across the snow. This method is called *ski jøring*. In modern times, ski jøring races are popular throughout Sápmi.

Below: A ski jøring race

Snow Scooters

In the 1960s, Sami reindeer herders started using snowmobiles in their work. Many Sami people ride snowmobiles—or "snow scooters" as they are called in Sápmi—just for fun. Some towns hold scooter races in winter and spring. Some races are just for kids.

Left: Participants in a lasso competition show how well they can throw lassos over reindeer antlers.

Above: Sami youths enjoy a game of indoor hockey. Universities and youth centers in Sápmi have modern facilities for sports like basketball, volleyball, and badminton too.

Soccer

In summertime, kids in Sápmi love to play soccer. The Sami even have their own soccer team that competes with other European teams. But since Sápmi is not a country with its own government, the team is not allowed in the International Federation of Football Association, which governs world soccer matches.

JOIKS!

Modern Sami sing the joik at parties and special occasions. Johan Turi, a herder from Kautokeino, wrote a book about the Sami in 1910. He said that a good joik singer could bring tears to listeners' eyes. Here are the words to a herder's joik about his reindeer. The joik tells about calving time, when reindeer calves are born:

Silken coated, silken coated, voia, voia, voia, nana, nana, nana,
Running like the sunbeams, voia, voia, voia, nana, nana, nana,
Small calves lowing, voia, voia, voia, nana, nana, nana,
Rushing . . . rushing, voia, voia, voia, nana, nana, nana, nana.

GLOSSARY

archaeologist: a scientist who studies past human cultures

Arctic Circle: an imaginary line circling the top of the earth at 23°28' south of the North Pole

discrimination: unfair treatment of a group of people, based on prejudice or hatred

earmark: a notch in an animal's ear that serves as a form of identification

fell: a rounded, treeless hill

fjord: a narrow bay that cuts into the coastline, often with mountains rising up on each side

gakti (GAHK-tee): a traditional Sami outfit

heathen: an insulting name for people who don't practice Christianity

insulation: material that provides protection from the cold

joik (yoyk): an old style of singing

lavvu (LAH-voo): a reindeer hide tent

lichen: a plant that grows on rocks and trees. It may be crusty, spongy, or hairy.

migrate: to travel to a new place, often in search of food or other resources

missionary: someone who tries to convert others to his or her religion

noaide (noh-AH-ee-deh): a spiritual leader similar to a shaman

nomad: someone who moves from place to place, without a settled home

parliament: a political group, elected by the people to speak on their behalf

permafrost: the soil of the tundra that remains frozen year-round

predator: an animal that survives by killing and eating other animals

sacrifice: an animal that is killed as an offering to a god

sii'da (see-EE-dah): a Sami community

ski jøring (skee YUH-reeng): a sport in which reindeer or dogs pull skiers quickly across the snow

summer solstice: the longest day of the year in the Northern Hemisphere, occurring on June 20, 21, or 22

taiga: the evergreen forests of the subarctic region

tundra: the treeless plains of the Arctic

FINDING OUT MORE

Books

Alexander, Bryan, and Cherry Alexander. *The Vanishing Arctic*. Charlotte, NC: Baker & Taylor, 1997.

Bullen, Susan. *People & Places: The Arctic & Its People*. New York: Raintree Steck-Vaughn Publishers, 1994.

Green, Jen. *Step Into: The Arctic World*. New York: Anness Publishing, 2000.

Lewin, Ted. *The Reindeer People*. New York: Simon & Schuster Children's Publishing, 1994.

Nazarri, Marco. *The Arctic World*. New York: Abbeville Press, 2000.

Parkison, Jami, and Andra Chase (illustrator). *Inger's Promise*. Shawnee Mission, KS: Marsh Media, 1995.

Rootes, David. *Endangered People & Places: The Arctic*. Minneapolis: Lerner Publishing Group, 1996.

Videos

Pathfinder (with subtitles). WinStar Home Video/Fox Lorber Films, 1988.

Sami Herders. Benchmark Films, Inc. (BENC), 1978.

Websites

<http://arcticcircle.uconn.edu /HistoryCulture/samiindex.html>

<http://home4.swipnet.se/~w-44111 /cwhome/cwsaami.html>

<http://www.itv.se/boreale /samieng.htm>

<http://www.saamiweb.org/english /magazine/children>

<http://www.sametinget.se/english /sapmi/index.html>

Organizations

The Saami Báiki Foundation
1430 32nd Street #2
West Oakland, CA 94608
Tel: 510/547-0350
E-mail: <saamibaiki@sinewave.com>
Website: <http://members.tripod.com /Baiki/index.html>

The Saami Council
FIN-99980 Ohcejohka/Utsjoki, Finland
Fax: (358) 16-677-353
E-mail: <samiradd@netti.fi>
Website: <http://www. saamicouncil.org>

INDEX

ABOUT THE AUTHOR

Deborah Robinson is a research fellow at Dartmouth College's Institute of Arctic Studies, where she works on projects involving reindeer, indigenous peoples' rights, and the environment. Deborah has traveled in Greenland, Finland, Sweden, and Norway.

PICTURE CREDITS

(B=bottom; I=inset; L=left; M=main; R=right; T=top)

Aanta Forsgren: 6M, 12M, 27T • B & C Alexander: 2, 3, 4M, 7I, 11B, 13T, 13B, 15I, 20M, 21B, 23T, 28M, 29I, 30I, 31I, 32M, 33R, 42M, 43T, 46 • Bo Holmberg: 14M, 18M, 25I, 40M • Camera Press: 5I, 7T, 8M, 9I, 24M • David Simson: 33T • Getty Images/Hulton Archive: 19T, 19B • Klingwalls Foto: 10, 17I, 27B, 35T, 35B, 36M, 41R, 41B • Lehtikuva Oy: 11T, 26M, 37T, 37I, 39B, 40R, 41T • Nik Wheeler: 9T, 17T, 23B, 26I, 29T, 30M, 34M, 39T, 47, 48 • Norrbottens Museum: 42I • North Wind Picture Archives: 16M • The Hutchison Library: 33I, 38M • Topham Picturepoint: 15T, 22M, 25T, 31T